GET THE FACTS
MATHS

Dr Bal Phondke has been a research scientist in BARC, the chief editor of *Science Today*, science editor of the *Times of India* group and the director of the National Institute of Science Communication. He is also a popular science writer with several books to his credit. He has won numerous awards, including the National Award and the Indira Gandhi Award.

In the same series

Get the Facts World
Soumyajit Mandal

Get the Facts India
Vaijayanti Savant Tonpe

Get the Facts Photography
Mukul Khattar

Get the Facts India
Vaijayanti Savant Tonpe

Get the Facts Grammar
Sankaranarayanan K.

Get the Facts Planet Earth
Biman Basu

Get the Facts Physics
Shobhit Mahajan

Get the Facts Quotes

Get the Facts Proverbs

Get the Facts
MATHS

Bal Phondke

SCHOLASTIC
New York Toronto London Auckland
Sydney New Delhi Hong Kong

This book was earlier published as *Maths in My Pocket*.
It was also published as *250 Maths Fun Facts* in January 2005.

Published by Scholastic India Pvt. Ltd.
A subsidiary of Scholastic Inc., New York, 10012 (USA).
Publishers since 1920, with international operations in Canada, Australia, New Zealand, the United Kingdom, India, and Hong Kong.

For information regarding permission, write to:
Scholastic India Pvt. Ltd.
Golf View Corporate Tower-A, 3rd Floor,
DLF Phase-V, Gurgaon-122002 (India)

Typeset by Mantra Virtual Services Pvt Ltd.

This edition: June 2010 April 2018

ISBN: 978-81-8477-592-1

Printed at RamPrintograph Delhi

Contents

Divisibility Rules

Any number that ends with an even number is divisible by 2.

Any number that ends with 0 or 5 is divisible by 5.

To know if a number is divisible by 11 subtract the sum of the odd digits from the sum of the even digits. If this leaves 0 or a number divisible by 11 then the original number is also divisible by 11.

For example, consider the number 2389. The sum of the odd digits (first and third) is 2 + 8 = 10 and the sum of the even digits (second and fourth) is 3 + 9 = 12. Subtracting 10 from 12 we get 2 which is not divisible by 11. So 2389 is not divisible by 11. But take 6567. The sum of the odd digits is 6 + 6 = 12 and that of the even digits is 5 + 7 = 12. Subtracting 12 from 12 we get 0. So 6567 is divisible by 11.

There is a simple test to find out if a number is divisible by 7.

Remove the last digit, double it, subtract it from the truncated original number and continue doing this until only one digit remains. If this is 0 or 7, then the original number is divisible by 7.

E.g. if the number is 1603; 160 – 2(3) = 154; 15 – 2(4) = 7, so 1603 is divisible by 7.

∞

There is another slightly more complicated test. Take the digits of the number in reverse order, from right to left, multiplying them successively by the digits 1, 3, 2, 6, 4, 5, repeating with this sequence of multipliers as long as necessary. Add the products. If this sum is a multiple of 7 then the original number is divisible by 7.

Example: Is 1603 divisible by 7?
3(1) + 0(3) + 6(2) + 1(6) = 21 is divisible by 7, so 1603 is too.

If the last three digits of a number X are divisible by 8, then X is too.

∞

If the sum of the digits of the number X is divisible by 9, then X is too.

∞

The rule to find out if a number is divisible by 13 is called L + 4M. The last digit of the number X has to be quadrupled and added to X without its last digit. For instance, if the number X you are testing is 345678, you would add 32 to 34567. Repeat this procedure until you get a number that you know for sure is or is not divisible by 13. If the number is divisible by 13, so is X.

∞

The rule to find out if a number is divisible by 17 is called L - 5M. This is similar to the rule for finding out divisibility by 13. Multiply the last digit of the number by

5 and then subtract it from the remaining number. This process must be repeated till we get a number that we are sure is or is not divisible by 17. The original number will also show the same property.

E.g. take the number 2363. 5 × 3 = 15. 236 – 15 = 221. Now 5 × 1 = 5 and 22 – 5 = 17. So 2363 is divisible by 17.

∞

The rule to find out divisibility by 19 is called L + 2M. This is similar to the rule for divisibility by 17. We multiply the last digit by 2 and subtract it from the rest of the number. We continue doing this till we get a number that is divisible by 19. Then the original number is also divisible by 19.

∞

If the sum of the digits of a number is divisible by 3, the number is also divisible by 3.

If the last two digits of a number form a number divisible by 4, the original number is also divisible by 4.

∞

If a number is divisible by both 3 and 2, then it is divisible by 6.

∞

If the number ends in 0, it is divisible by 10.

∞

To find out if a number is divisible by 13, delete the last digit from the number, then subtract 9 times the deleted digit from the rest of the number. If the number obtained is divisible by 13, then so is the original number. E.g. the last digit of 351 is 1. If we delete it we get 35. Now if $9 \times 1 = 9$ is subtracted from 35 we get 26, which is divisible by 13. So 351 is also divisible by 13.

The History of Numbers

A number is an abstract concept. A numeral is a way of writing down or talking about a number.

∞

Counting is nearly as old as speech and numerals are as old as writing.

∞

Numbers were 'invented' or 'discovered', depending on one's philosophical viewpoint, long before history. This happened when people realised that they could think about 'how many' without needing to know 'how many WHAT?' and that there is an idea of number that is separate from the world of things that can be counted.

∞

The word for the number 1 in various European languages has the letter 'n' in it. The word 'number' most probably originated from the Latin word '*unos*'.

At first, only numbers upto 10 were known and used. Objects more than 10 were counted in terms of how many were left after counting upto 10. In fact the English words eleven and twelve are forms of very old English words meaning one left and two left respectively.

∞

The German words *elf* and *zwelf* or the French words *onz* and *douz* are also similar in nature.

∞

Numbers were invented before writing was. So, initially there were no written symbols for numbers.

∞

The Sumerians who occupied the fertile land between the two mighty rivers, Tigris and Euphrates, invented writing. They also invented the first symbols for writing down numbers.

Some of the oldest evidence of counting so far discovered comes from ancient artefacts belonging to groups of hunters and gatherers. For example, a wolf bone dated about 30,000 BC, has been discovered with a series of notches carved in it, which seem to represent a tally of some kind.

∞

There are cultures that have number systems consisting only of words for one, two, and many. Certain Australian aboriginal tribes use this system.

∞

The words for three in some European languages are very similar to the words for beyond or over. E.g. the word for three in Latin is *tres*, which is similar to the word meaning beyond, *trans*. This indicates that people speaking these languages only knew numbers up to 2. Anything more than 2 was 'beyond' or 'many'.

This one, two, many system has been extended by some cultures to form the 2-system. This allows representation of groups of three or four objects by repeating the words for one or two. Thus, three would be two-one, and four would be two-two. This is the origin of the binary system.

∞

The development of ordinal numbers (first, second, third, etc.) from cardinal numbers (one, two, three, etc.) may have happened as a result of finger counting. Fingers, and sometimes toes, can be used to count on. If this is always done in the same order, then the same finger will always be used to represent the same number. For example, the ring finger of the right hand might always denote the number 7. This provides a correlation between the 7 items being counted and the 7th finger in the sequence.

Numbers and Civilisations

A. Arabic Numbers

The Arabic system of arithmetic is based on the Indian numerals and arithmetic system. The system later travelled to Europe.

∞

In the eleventh century, three different systems of arithmetic were in practice in Arab countries. In the first system, 'finger-arithmetic', numbers were counted on fingers, with the numerals written entirely in words. This system was used by the business community. The second system, the sexagesimal, used numerals denoted by letters of the Arabic alphabet. The third system used arithmetic with Indian numerals and fractions with the decimal place-value system.

∞

As early as the seventh century, the Indian number system was known and used in areas that soon became part of the Arab world. The system came to be known as 'arithmetic of the nine symbols', because in the Indian decimal system any number could be expressed in terms of the digits 1 to 9 and 0.

It is believed that the mathematician Al-Khwarizmi wrote the first Arabic text to explain the Indian number system. His Arabic original is lost, but a Latin translation *'Algoritmi de numero Indorum'* (Al-Khwarizmi on the Hindu Art of Reckoning) done in the twelfth century, still exists.

While the Latin text is believed to differ somewhat from the original, it does describe the Indian place-value system based on the digits 1 through 9, and 0, and the first use of zero as a place holder in positional base notation.

The word 'algorithm', which is the basis of modern computer science, derives from the Latin translation of Al Khwarizmi's name *Algoritmi*.

∞

The Arabs initially adopted the Indian method of using a dust board to calculate. Indian numerals were even known by the term '*guba*' or '*ghubar*' from the Arabic word for dust. A dust board made it easy to move the numbers around or erase some of them during calculation, much in the same way that a blackboard is used with chalk and eraser.

∞

The earliest surviving Arabic book that presents the Indian system is the *Kitab al-fusul fi al-hisab al-Hindi* by Al-Uqlidisi, written sometime in the middle of the tenth century.

∞

The requirement of dust boards had been the obstacle in using the Indian system, as Arabs preferred to use a simpler system that required only parts of the body, such as fingers and toes.

∞

Al-Uqlidisi came up with new ways of calculating with Indian symbols, using pen and paper, which previously required dust boards.

∞

Even though the Indian system was used by many scholars, the business community continued to use 'finger-arithmetic'. Abu'l-Wafa, despite being an expert on Indian numerals, wrote a book on the Arabic finger-arithmetic, using Arab letter numerals.

∞

The numerals in the old Arabic system

were represented by letters, but not in the order of the dictionary. The system, known as *huruf al jumal* meaning 'letters for calculating' or as *abjad* which are the first four numbers (1 = a, 2 = b, j = 3, d = 4), had the numbers 1 to 9 represented by the first nine letters (a to i); the numbers 10, 20, 30, ... 90 by the next nine letters; 100, 200, ... 900 represented by the next set of letters and so on. The 28 Arabic letters were assigned to these numbers and the one left-over letter represented 1000. The base 60 notation of the *abjadi* Arabic letter system was used by Arabs in astronomy.

B. Babylonian Numbers

The number system of the Babylonians was derived from those of the Sumerians and the Akkadians. The base 60 notation, known as the sexagesimal system, evolved from these earlier number systems.

The base 60 system used a combination of two symbols—a 'unit' symbol and a 'tens' symbol to represent numbers 1 to 59. Thus if the symbol *x* represented 1 and the symbol *y* represented 10, then 2 would be *xx* and 11 would be *yx*.

The numbers 1 to 59, thus represented, were placed in the rightmost position. For numbers over 60, the leftmost position was used, with a value of *n* x 60, for any digit *n* (from 1 to 59) placed there. Thus the number 72 would be represented as *x yx* (i.e. 1 x 60 + 11). The system had problems—the sexagesimal numbers 61 and 2 had almost the same notation; and there was no zero to place in an empty position. Using a space solved the problem, but not when it came to numbers that had the same depiction, like 60 and 1. The space also caused problems in working with fractions.

∞

There are several theories on why the base 60 was used, but none that are conclusive. One theory assumes that 60 being the smallest number divisible by 1, 2, 3, 4, 5 and 6, it maximised the number of divisors. A base of 12 was also used by many civilisations, as several measures of money, length and weight even now involve 12.

∞

Babylonians inscribed numbers and symbols with a stylus on wet clay. The stylus formed wedge shaped marks, and this led to the cuneiform system of writing (*cuneus* meaning wedge and *forma* meaning shape). The Babylonians came up with the system of dividing a day into 24 hours, each hour into 60 minutes and each minute into 60 seconds; a form of counting still in use after 4000 years!

∞

They also constructed tables to aid calculation. Two tablets found, dating from 2000 BC give squares of numbers up

to 59 and cubes of numbers up to 32.
E.g. 8^2 = 1,4(in base 60)
i.e. 8^2 = 1,4 = 1x60 + 4 = 64

C. Chinese Numbers

The earliest Chinese number system used a number of symbols to represent numbers and was based on the decimal system. The system was additive, and not positional, so there was no need for a zero. A number 2437 would be represented by the symbol for 2000, followed by that for 400, that for 30 and then by the symbol for 7.

∞

Around the fourth century the Chinese discovered a method that used counting-boards. A counting board is a checker board with rows and columns. In a row, a number was formed placing rods representing units in the right-most column; those representing tens in the next column to the left; rods for hundreds in the column next to it and so forth. The most significant property was that it was a natural place value system. Zero was still not represented, but was depicted by leaving a blank square on the board. To multiply by 10, 100 or 1000, for instance, rods on the board were moved to the left by 1, 2 and 3 squares and to divide by 10, 100 or 1000, rods were moved to the left by 1,2 or 3 squares, and so on.

∞

The Chinese invented the abacus around the fourteenth century. Very similar to the counting board, the abacus used beads sliding on a wire to represent numbers, instead of rods. The abacus could be used to add, subtract, multiply, divide, and even calculate square roots and cube roots.

∞

The abacus is still used in modern day China, and is often considered faster than western calculators when dealing with large numbers.

D. Egyptian Numbers

Egyptians had a writing system as early as 3000 BC. It was based on hieroglyphs, which were small pictures or pictographs, representing words.

They had a base 10 system of hieroglyphs meant for numerals: there were distinct symbols to represent one unit, one ten, one hundred, one thousand ... till one million or 10 to the power of 6.

Hieroglyphs also accommodated fractions, although only unit fractions, with the exceptions of the frequently used 2/3 and 3/4. Fraction was represented by a symbol.

The Egyptians evolved three writing systems: the hieroglyphic, the hieratic and the demotic. The hieroglyphic was treated as the sacred writing, mostly written on stone and reserved for formal inscriptions.

∞

Numeral hieroglyphs constantly evolved over the two thousand years of the ancient Egyptian civilisation.

∞

Once the Egyptians invented papyrus to write on, they developed a number system consisting of 'hieratic' numerals. They allowed numbers to be written in a compact form, but they had separate symbols for each number, so there were a large number of symbols to memorise. The system had separate symbols for numbers 1 to 9, 10 to 90, 100 to 900 and 1000 to 9000.

Hieratic script, also known as temple writing, was used for record-keeping by priests and scribes, and mostly for writing on papyrus.

∞

Demotic writing evolved from the hieratic. It was a cursive script, and was used in everyday life.

∞

If a positive whole number is represented as a sum of unit fractions not consisting entirely of 1s, then the sum of the denominators in the unit fractions is called an Egyptian number. Eg: 1/2 + 1/3 + 1/6 =1 and so 2+3+6=11 is an Egyptian number.

∞

The Egyptian number system was based on unit fractions. Numbers like 1/7 were easily represented, and those like 2/7 could be represented as sums of unit fractions. 2/7= 1/4 + 1/28. But one could not use the same fractions twice, while representing another number: so 2/7= 1/7 + 1/7 was not permitted. A formula that represents a sum of distinct unit fractions is called an Egyptian fraction.

E. Greek Numbers

The first of the Greek number systems to evolve was the *acrophonic system* in use in the first millennium BC. 'Acrophonic' means that the symbols representing the numerals are derived from the first letter of the name of the number, so the symbol comes from an abbreviation of the word used for the number.

The exception was the number one, the symbol for which was a plain '|' which was not derived from the number's initial letter.

These numbers were also known as Herodian numbers. Herod was a second century writer who described the numbers. They were also known as Attic numbers, since they occur in Attic inscriptions.

∞

The system had no symbol for zero. Since the system was not a positionally notated one, there was no need for a zero to indicate an empty place.

∞

The form of the number varied, depending on what the number stood for or referred to. For example, the numbers that were used to represent money were different from those that were used to represent, say, the fruits bought with the money.

∞

Another Greek number system was that consisting of alphabetical numerals, also known as the 'learned' system.

∞

In the alphabetical system, values were given to the letters of the alphabet, and these alphabets were then used to indicate the numerals that they thus represented. Such a system of writing based on alphabets was first used by the Greeks, but it was invented by the Phoenicians.

∞

The first nine letters were assigned to represent numbers 1 to 9; the next nine as symbols for 10, 20, ... 90 and so on. Sometimes a bar was placed over the symbol, to distinguish it from the actual letter.

∞

This system could represent numbers up to 999. To represent numbers between 1000 and 9000, a superscript was added to the symbols for numbers 1 to 9. Thus A with a superscript i was 1000.

To represent numbers above 9999, they used the symbol myriad M which represented 10,000. The symbol M with a small numeral (upto 999) written above it as a superscript would mean that the small numeral is to be multiplied by 10,000.

F. Hebrew Numbers

The Hebrew number system, like many others, used the letters of the alphabet as numerical symbols. The first letter represented 1, the second 2, the tenth 10, the eleventh 20 and so on. The 22 letters of the Jewish alphabet represented numbers till 400. Zero was not represented.

In the Jewish holy book, the Talmud,

numbers greater than 400 are created by composition. E.g. 500 = 400+100 and 700 = 400+300.

In Hebrew, numbers are gendered. Thus in the expression 'two men' two would be *shney,* while in 'two women' two would be *shtey.*

G. Incan Numbers

The Incas came up with a way to count and record numerical information which did not require them to write. It consisted of tying knots in strings, called *quipu.*

The *quipu* is made up of strings with knots in it that represented numbers, using a positional base 10 notation. If the number 234 was to be recorded on the *quipu,* then four touching knots were placed near the free end of the string (in the units position), a space was left, then three touching knots for the 10s, another space, and finally 2 touching knots for the 100s. To represent a larger number, more knot-groups were used, one for each power of 10.

∞

The system had a zero notation, indicated by no knots in that position. So that the space indicating zero was not confused with the space between place value positions, the spacing between knots had to be regular and accurate.

Different colours were used to identify the different objects recorded on the strings. A particular coloured string indicated what the numbers recorded on it were for. For instance, brown string might be used for recording the numbers of cows, and white for the number of goats.

∞

The meanings were often concrete, like the knots in a particular coloured string indicating the number of cattle. But often they were abstract, and a string of a specific colour might indicate 'peace'. *Quipucamayocs*, or keepers of the knots, were appointed by the Inca king. As government statisticians, the *quipucamayocs* kept official census records, records of produce, animals, weapons and so on, of the town.

∞

The Incas also came up with a counting board, known as the *yupana*. While some believe it's the Peruvian abacus, its method of use is still unclear.

H. Indian Numbers

The simple but ingenious idea of expressing every number using a set of ten symbols, where each symbol possesses a place value and an absolute value, originated in India. It made calculation easy and gave us the concept of arithmetic as we know it today.

∞

Indian mathematicians wrote several treatises between 1000 BC and 1000 AD, that introduced the concepts of zero, the techniques of algorithm and algebra, square root and cube root.

∞

An important aspect of the Indian numbers system is the appearance of the numbers 0, 1, 2, 3, 4, 5, 6, 7, 8 and 9 and how they have evolved into the form used today, several millennia on.

∞

A second, even more important feature is the introduction of the place value system and the base 10 notation evolved by Indian mathematicians – concepts essential to modern arithmetic, algorithm and higher branches of mathematics. The place value system had numerals, which depending on their value, stood in different positions relative to the other numerals. The modern place-value system is directly derived from this one.

∞

The Arab mathematician Al-Biruni, already familiar with Indian astronomy and mathematics from Arabic translations of Sanskrit texts, visited India and made a detailed study of Indian sciences, mathematics and philosophy. He wrote several books on these subjects. His work throws light on early Indian achievements in these fields and records the level of advancement. In these books, he speaks of the difference between the number systems used in the Arab world and by the Indians. He says while the Arabs used letters to denote numbers, the Indians did not do so. Instead they had separate symbols for them, with considerable variation across the country.

The origin of the Indian symbols for numerals is believed to be the Brahmi numerals, developed around the third century BC. Believed to have evolved from an earlier alphabetic numeral system, they then gave way to numerals in the Gupta period, which lasted between the fourth and sixth century AD.

∞

From the Gupta numerals came the Nagari or Devanagari numerals. Devanagari was considered a beautiful script. It literally meant 'writing of the gods', and developed between the seventh and eleventh century AD.

∞

It is variously believed that the Indians devised the positional place value system influenced by the Chinese system or the Babylonian base 60 system or entirely by themselves because they wanted a system to deal with very large numbers, which historians claim they were fascinated by.

∞

The oldest dated Indian document containing a number written with the place-value notation which we know today, is a legal document from 594 AD.

∞

The mathematician Aryabhatta is said to have devised a number system in 500 AD which did not have a zero but was still a positional system. He coined a word 'kha' for position, which came to be used later as the name for zero. Several earlier Indian manuscripts used a dot to denote an empty place in positional notation.

∞

The use of zero as a number came into Indian mathematics around 650 AD. The zero was used to denote an empty place in the base 10 place-value system.

Although the Indian idea of zero and Indian mathematics spread to China and to the Arab world, it was the Italian mathematician Fibonacci who introduced these number systems to Europe in his books *Liber Abaci* in 1202 AD, describing the nine Indian symbols and zero. But in the late 1200s and 1300s only Roman numerals were permitted to be used in parts of Italy. Only by the fifteenth century did European tradesman, surveyors and merchants begin using the Indo-Arabic numerals.

∞

Zero, apart from being a numeral, is also a concept of nothingness or emptiness and the study of it had deep philosophical underpinnings. In ancient times, it was called *pujyam* and when it was used in computation, it was represented by a dot. This term is still used, along with the more current *shunyam* meaning blank or void.

Indians termed the concept of void *shukla* or *shubra,* which influenced the Arab term *siphra* for zero. This term in turn directly influenced the English term cipher, which means zero.

∞

Indian mathematician Brahmagupta first put forth the concept of zero in the seventh century treatise *Brahmasputa-siddhanta* which enumerated rules for computation with zero, and also spoke of negative numbers. This text was translated into Arabic as the *Zij-al-Sind Hind.*

∞

This translation was used as the standard reference text by mathematicians and others in the Arab world. It was from this text, the translation of Brahmagupta's work on Indian mathematics, that mathematicians in the Arab world worked on and perfected the decimal system, giving to the world the Arab numerals, which are still in use today.

I. Mayan Numbers

The ancient Mayans in central America, used three symbols – a dot, a bar and a symbol for zero (or completion), to devise an advanced counting system that could represent very large numbers.

∞

The Mayans used place values, like in the Indian numbering system, to be able to express very large numbers. They differed from the Indian place value system, in that they arranged the place values vertically and used a more complicated base 20 notation.

∞

The Mayans' use of zero goes back much earlier than the time of devising the place value system. They were well-versed in this advanced number system while Europe still struggled with the Roman numeral system.

∞

The Mayans counted on their fingers and toes, adding up to 20, which is believed to have been the reason for their base 20 system. They also had two calendars, one with 260 days and the other with 365 days.

∞

The Mayans were extremely interested in astronomy and carried out astronomical measurements with the help of sticks. With crude instruments like the sticks and a surviving observatory believed to have been built by them, the Mayans calculated accurately the length of the year as 365.242 days, which is astoundingly close to the modern value of 365.242198 days.

J. Roman Numbers

We still use Roman numerals to indicate order of persons (John II, Elizabeth II); in publishing, or where we use Latin numerical words like duo, decade etc. But for numbers, we now use the Arabic numerals and not the Roman numerals. The biggest difference between Roman numerals and Arabic ones is that the former did not have a symbol for zero.

∞

1, 2 and 3 were indicated by the same symbol, repeated as many times as needed – I, II, III. Instead of adding little marks to denote the next number, the Romans devised a symbol 'V' for 5. They placed a number I in front of it, to indicate subtraction and so IV became the symbol for 4, by subtracting 1 from 5. Similarly, they placed I after V to indicate 6 (VI), placed II after V to indicate 7(VII) and so on till 8(VIII).

The symbol for 10 was X. Therefore 9 was represented by IX. Placing a smaller number in front of a larger number meant subtracting the smaller number from the larger one, and placing it after the larger number meant adding it to the larger one.

L was the symbol for 50. Therefore, by placing the symbol for 10(X) in front of it, the symbol for 40(XL) could be explained. 60 was LX, 70 was LXX and 80 was LXXX.

D was the symbol for 500. Therefore 400 would be CD. A number like 448 would be represented by CDXLVIII and the number 999 would be written as CMXCIX. As this system was too cumbersome and confusing, the Arab numerals were adopted for modern numeral representation.

Romans counted on their fingers; the symbols I, II and III are visual representations of 1, 2 and 3 fingers held up respectively. V came to be chosen as the symbol for 5, because of the shape 'V' formed between the thumb and little finger, when the hand is held up, palm outstretched to denote 5.

The Latin word for 100 was *centum* and for 1000 was *Mille*. Therefore, C and M were the chosen symbols for 100 and 1000 respectively, in the Roman numeral system.

Personalities and Numbers

The sequence of numbers 0, 1, 1, 2, 3, 5, 8, 13, 21, is very famous. Except the first two, every number in this sequence is the sum of the preceding two numbers. Such numbers are called Fibonacci numbers.

∞

153 is a very special number because $153 = 1^3 + 5^3 + 3^3$. Such numbers are called Armstrong numbers. Some other Armstrong numbers are 370, 371, 407. 153 is also equal to 1 + 2 + 3 + 4 + 5 + 6 + 7 + 8 + 9 + 10 + 11 + 12 + 13 + 14 + 15 + 16 + 17.

∞

1729 is a very special number. When the self-taught Indian mathematical genius Srinivasa Ramanujan was dying of tuberculosis, the mathematician G. H. Hardy often visited him. According to C. P. Snow, it was on one of these visits that the following occurred:

'Hardy used to visit him, as he lay

dying in hospital at Putney. It was on one of those visits that the incident of the taxicab number took place. Hardy had gone out to Putney by taxi, his usual method conveyance. He went into the room where Ramanujan lay in bed. Hardy, always inept at introducing a conversation, said, with no preamble whatsoever, "The number of my taxicab was 1729. It seemed to me rather a dull number." To which Ramanujan replied, "No Hardy! No! It is a very interesting number. It is the smallest number expressible as the sum of two cubes in two different ways." '

Such numbers are, therefore, known after Ramanujan as Ramanujan numbers. Some other Ramanujan numbers are 4104, 13832, 20683, 32832.

∞

9 is a very interesting number $9^2 = 81$ and $8 + 1 = 9$. Similarly $297^2 = 88,209$ and $88 + 209 = 297$. Such numbers are known as Kaprekar numbers after the Indian mathematician D. R. Kaprekar who

discovered these properties. Some other Kaprekar numbers are 1, 45, 55, 99, 703.

∞

D. R. Kaprekar is also known for a process called *Kaprekar's Operation*. Take a four-digit number, in which all four digits are not the same, and rearrange the digits to get the largest and smallest numbers they can form. Then extract the smaller number from the larger one. If you continue the process, you will always reach the number 6174. Let us illustrate this with an example. Take the number 3289.

Step 1: 9832 - 2389 = 7443
Step 2: 7443 - 3447 = 3996
Step 3: 9963 - 3699 = 6264
Step 4: 6642 - 2466 = 4176
Step 5: 7641 - 1467 = 6174

If we continue the process we would of course, keep repeating the line 7641 - 1467 = 6174. Thus, the number 3289 took 5 steps to reach the magic number 6174. Not all numbers take five steps, however, some take more, some take less. Such numbers are also called Kaprekar numbers. Many of these numbers end up in 6174. That is why it is called the Kaprekar constant.

∞

A positive integer which is divisible by the sum of its digits, is called a Harshad number. It is also called a Niven number or a multi-digital number. The first few are 1, 2, 3, 4, 5, 6, 7, 8, 9, 10, 12, 18, 20, 21, 24. E.g. the sum of the digits of the number 21 is 2 + 1 = 3 and 21 is divisible by 3.

∞

Nayan Hajratwala, a participant in the Great Internet Mersenne Prime Search (GIMPS), has discovered the first known million-digit prime number. The prime number $2^{6,972,593} - 1$, contains 2098960 digits.

∞

A magic square is one where the sum of numbers in each row and each column is the same. In some magic squares the sum of both the diagonals are also the same. Benjamin Franklin discovered a unique magic square where the sum of numbers in all the rows and columns is 260. Also the sum of each half column and half row is 130. It also has other patterns where the sum is 260. This is known as the Benjamin Franklin magic square.

52	61	4	13	20	29	36	45
14	3	62	51	46	35	30	19
53	60	5	12	21	28	37	44
11	6	59	54	43	38	27	22
55	58	7	10	23	26	39	42
9	8	57	56	41	40	25	24
50	63	2	15	18	31	34	47
16	1	64	49	48	33	32	17

The sum of numbers in the above squares of the same pattern-fills is also 260.

∞

The prime numbers 3, 5, 7 form an arithmetic sequence. There is a constant difference of 2 between one prime and the next. However, the next term of the sequence is 9, which is not a prime number. So, this arithmetic sequence consists of three consecutive prime numbers.

The primes 5, 11, 17, 23, 29 form an arithmetic sequence with a constant difference of 6. The next term 35 is not prime, but five consecutive prime numbers forming an arithmetic sequence beats three consecutive prime numbers! So what's the world record? If you start with the prime 100996972469714247637786655587969840329509324689190041803603417758 904341703348882159067229719 and use a constant difference of 210 you will produce the record-breaking arithmetic sequence of 10 primes discovered by Manfred Toplic on March 2, 1998.

∞

28 has a special property:
$28 = 1^3 + 3^3$. That is, it is the sum of the cubes of the first two odd numbers.

The number 28 is a special number for another reason as well. Its factors are 1, 2, 4, 7 and 14. They add up to 28. Such numbers are called perfect numbers. Other perfect numbers are 6, 496, 8128 and so on. N. J. Sloane invented a complex formula to find such perfect numbers.

∞

Usually, by reversing any number and adding it to the original one it is possible to get a palindromic number after a few steps.

E.g. 64 + 46 = 110

110 + 011 = 121, which is a palindromic number. It reads the same forwards or backwards. E.g.

79 + 97 = 176
176 + 671 = 847
847 + 748 = 1595
1595 + 5951 = 7546
7546 + 6457 = 14003
14003 + 30014 = 44044

This is a palindrome. The first number took just 2 steps and the second, 5 steps.

But 196 is an exception as John Walker discovered on May 2, 1990. In spite of employing a computer programme to carry out this process of reversal and addition he had to abandon the effort after 2,415,836 steps that yielded a number with one million digits. Still there was no palindrome.

Here is a remarkable pattern of numbers known as Pascal's triangle.

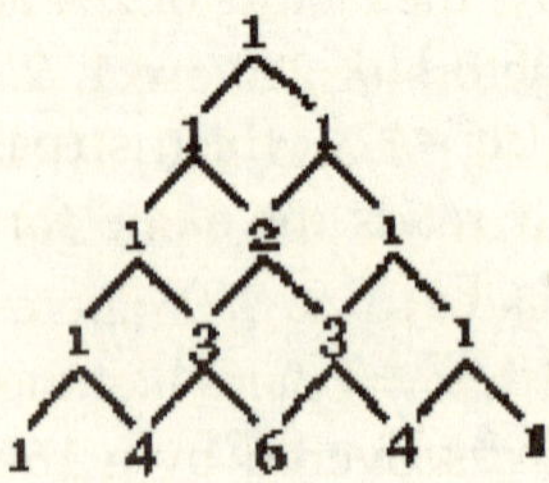

Every successive rung from the top gives the various powers of 11. The top is 11^0, the next is 11^1, the next is 11^2 and so on. It also gives the coefficients of every term in the equation $(x + y)^n$.

Every even number greater than 2 is a sum of two prime numbers. Thus, 4 = 2 + 2; 6 = 3 + 3; 8 = 3 + 5; 10 = 3 + 7 and so on. This was observed by Goldbach in 1742 and is now known as the Goldbach conjecture.

∞

A few pairs of numbers have a peculiar affinity for each other and are called 'amicable numbers.' For instance the pair of 220 and 284. All the factors of 220, i.e., those less than itself, add up to 284 and, surprisingly, the factors of 284 add up to 220. The factors of 220 are 1, 2, 4, 5, 10, 11, 20, 22, 44, 55 and 110. Their sum is 284. Likewise, the factors of 284 – 1, 2, 4, 71 and 142 add up to 220. There are only three other known pairs like these, 1,184 and 1,210, discovered by a 16-year-old Italian named Nicolo Paganini, 17,296 and 18,416, and the large pair 9,363,584 and 9,437,056.

∞

The sequence of numbers 1, 3, 4, 7, 11, 18, 29, 47, 76, 123, form a companion to the numbers in the Fibonacci series. Each number in the sequence is a sum of the previous two numbers. This sequence is attributed to Lucas and is known as the Lucas numbers.

∞

A composite number, the sum of whose digits is the sum of the digits of its prime factors, is called a Smith number. One example of the Smith number is the familiar 666, which is also known as the beast number. The prime factors of 666 are 2, 3, 3 and 37.

Now 6 + 6 + 6 = 18 and

2 + 3 + 3 + 3 + 7 = 18.

Another Smith number is 4937775.

∞

A number of the form $C_n = 2^n n + 1$ is called a Cullen number. The first few Cullen numbers are 3, 9, 25, 65, 161, 385. E.g. for $n = 1$, $(2^1 \times 1) + 1 = 2 + 1 = 3$.

Like the Armstrong number 153 which is $= 1^3 + 5^3 + 3^3$, 175 is an interesting number because
$175 = 1^1 + 7^2 + 5^3$.

∞

The symbol ∞ had been used as an alternative to M in Roman numerals until 1655, when John Wallis suggested it be used to denote infinity instead.

∞

A Keith number is an *n*-digit integer. *N* such that if a Fibonacci-like sequence (in which each term in the sequence is the sum of the *n* previous terms) is formed with the first *n* terms being the digits of the number *N*, then *N* itself occurs as a term in the sequence. E.g. 197 is a Keith number since it generates the sequence 1, 9, 7, 17, 33, 57, 107, 197 ...

The sequence of numbers 1, 4, 11, 16, 24, 29, 33, 35, 39 is obtained by noting the position of the letter 't' in the sentence defining it: '**t** is **t**he firs**t**, four**t**h, eleven**t**h, six**t**een**t**h ... letter of this sequence.' This is known as Aronson's sequence.

∞

A Carol number is a number of the form $4^k - 2^{k+1} - 1$ or $(2^k - 1)^2 - 2$. For $k = 1, 2, 3$ ... the Carol numbers are – 1, 7, 47.

∞

A Friedman number is a positive integer which can be written in some non-trivial way using its own digits, together with the symbols +, –, ×, ÷ or exponents. E.g. $25 = 5^2$ and $126 = 21 \times 6$. All Friedman numbers with 4 or fewer digits are known. They were found through a computer search. The first few are 25, 121, 125, 126, 127, 128, 153, 216, 289, 343, 347, 625, 688, 736, 1022, 1024.

A number of the form $M^n = 2^n - 1$, where *n* is an integer is known as a Mersenne number. E.g. for n = 3, $2^3 - 1 = 8 - 1 = 7$. The first few Mersenne numbers are 1, 3, 7, 15, 31, 63, 127, 255.

∞

A Proth number is a number of the form $N = k \times 2^n + 1$ where *k* is an odd number, *n* is a positive integer, and $2^n > k$. The first few Proth numbers are 3, 5, 9, 13, 17, 25, 33, 41, 49, 57, 65. The Cullen numbers are a special case of the Proth numbers where *k* = n.

∞

When *k* = 1, they are called Fermont numbers. A Sierpinski number of the first kind is a number of the form $S^n = n^n + 1$. E.g. for n = 3, $3^3 + 1 = 27 + 1 = 28$. The first few are 2, 5, 28, 257, 3126, 46657, 823544, 16777217.

A Thâbit ibn Kurrah number is a number of the form $K_n = 3 \times 2^n - 1$. The first few for $n = 0, 1, 2 \ldots$ are 2, 5, 11 ...

∞

A Pythagorean triple is a trio of positive integers a, b, c such that they satisfy the Pythagorean equation $a^2 + b^2 = c^2$. The first such triple is 3, 4, 5 because $3^2 = 9$, $4^2 = 16$, and $9 + 16 = 25 = 5^2$. Others are 5, 12, 13; 7, 24, 25; 9, 40, 41. It is interesting to note that such triples contain a sequence of one odd number and two other consecutive numbers.

∞

There is a simple formula that gives all the Pythagorean triples. Suppose that m and n are two positive integers, with $m < n$. Then $n^2 - m^2$, $2mn$, and $n^2 + m^2$ make a Pythagorean triple.

∞

A Woodall number is of the form $W_n = 2^n n - 1$. The first few are 1, 7, 23, 63, 159, 383. The first few *n* for which the Woodall number W_n is a prime number are 2, 3, 6, 30, 75, 81, corresponding to the Woodall numbers 7, 23, 383, 32212254719, 2833419889721787128217599.

Special Features

The Pythagorean triple 3, 4, 5 is related as $3^2 + 4^2 = 5^2$. But there is another relationship $3^3 + 4^3 + 5^3 = 6^3$

∞

We all know of the Pyramids in Egypt. Some numbers also have a tendency to build pyramids. E.g.

$$1^2 = 1$$
$$2^2 = (1 + 1)^2 = 1 + 2 + 1$$
$$3^2 = (1 + 1 + 1)^2 = 1 + 2 + 3 + 2 + 1$$
$$4^2 = (1 + 1 + 1 + 1)^2 = 1 + 2 + 3 + 4 + 3 + 2 + 1$$

∞

Here is another interesting pyramid:

$$1^2 = 1$$
$$11^2 = 121$$
$$111^2 = 12321$$
$$1111^2 = 1234321$$

The 9 digits 1 to 9 tend to get together and form some delightful patterns. Thus,

$$12 \times 483 = 5796$$
$$27 \times 198 = 5346$$
$$42 \times 138 = 5796$$
$$39 \times 186 = 7254$$

The number 7 displays a very curious property. It forms a very different kind of pyramid:

$$1 \times 7 + 3 = 10$$
$$14 \times 7 + 2 = 100$$
$$142 \times 7 + 6 = 1000$$
$$1428 \times 7 + 4 = 10000$$
$$14285 \times 7 + 5 = 100000$$
$$142857 \times 7 + 1 = 1000000$$
$$1428571 \times 7 + 3 = 10000000$$
$$14285714 \times 7 + 2 = 100000000$$
$$142857142 \times 7 + 6 = 1000000000$$
$$1428571428 \times 7 + 4 = 10000000000$$

That is why the decimal expansion of 1/7 has the repeating sequence 142857. In other words 1/7 = 0.142857142857 endlessly.

123321 and 2002 are numbers that read the same forwards as well as backwards. Such numbers are called palindromic numbers. Starting with any number one can get a palindromic number by following this simple method:

$$96 + 69 = 165$$
$$165 + 561 = 726$$
$$726 + 627 = 1353$$
$$1353 + 3531 = 4884$$

which is palindromic.

∞

Here are two special pyramids.

1	1
1 + 3	3 + 5
1 + 3 + 5	7 + 9 + 11
1 + 3 + 5 + 7	13 + 15 + 17 + 19
1 + 3 + 5 + 7 + 9	21 + 23 + 25 + 27 + 29

The total of numbers in every rung of the first pyramid is a square. It is called a square pyramid. Likewise, the second pyramid is a cubic pyramid because every rung adds up to a cube.

The number 7 has shown a peculiar trait. The number 9 is not far behind.

$$1 \times 9 + 2 = 11$$
$$12 \times 9 + 3 = 111$$
$$123 \times 9 + 4 = 1111$$
$$1234 \times 9 + 5 = 11111$$
$$12345 \times 9 + 6 = 111111$$

37 is another astonishing number:
$3 \times 37 = 111$ and $1 + 1 + 1 = 3$
$6 \times 37 = 222$ and $2 + 2 + 2 = 6$
$9 \times 37 = 333$ and $3 + 3 + 3 = 9$
and so on.

Starting with 7 we come across another special feature :

7 is a prime number
73 is a prime number
739 is a prime number
7393 is a prime number
73939 is a prime number
739391 is a prime number
7393913 is a prime number
73939133 is a prime number

Start with any positive integer and obtain a sequence of numbers by following these rules:
First, if the current number is even, divide it by two; if it is odd, multiply it by three and add one.
Second, repeat.

Let's try a few numbers to see what happens:

n = 3; 10, 5, 16, 8, 4, 2, 1, 4, 2, 1, ...
n = 4; 2, 1, 4, 2, 1, ...
n = 5; 16, 8, 4, 2, 1, 4, 2, 1, ...
n = 6; 3, 10, 5, 16, 8, 4, 2, 1, 4, 2, 1, ...
n = 7; 22, 11, 34, 17, 52, 26, 13, 40, 20, 10, 5, 16, 8, 4, 2, 1, 4, 2, 1, ...

This has been found to be true of any number. Sequences that bounce up and down and repeat are called hailstone numbers.

∞

666 is a very strange number with many special features.

$666 = 3^6 - 2^6 + 1^6$

$666 = 6^3 + 6^3 + 6^3 + 6 + 6 + 6$

That is not all. It has another set of special properties.

$$666 = 2^2 + 3^2 + 5^2 + 7^2 + 11^2 + 13^2 + 17^2$$

Every number on the right hand side of the above equation is a prime number.

∞

The number 9 never fails to amaze with its curious properties.

$$9 \times 9 + 7 = 88$$
$$98 \times 9 + 6 = 888$$
$$987 \times 9 + 5 = 8888$$
$$9876 \times 9 + 4 = 88888$$

There is more to the number 9:

$$9 \times 9 = 81$$
$$99 \times 99 = 9801$$
$$999 \times 999 = 998001$$
$$9999 \times 9999 = 99980001$$

∞

The formula $n^2 - n + 41$ where n is an integer results in a prime number.

For $n = 1$, $1^2 - 1 + 41 = 41$

For $n = 2$, $2^2 - 2 + 41 = 43$

For $n = 3$, $3^2 - 3 + 41 = 47$

For $n = 4$, $4^2 - 4 + 41 = 53$

Number 41, 43, 47, 53... are all prime numbers.

∞

Start with any number. Find the square of the digits in that number and add them. This forms the next number in the sequence. Continue in the same fashion. If the number 1 appears in the sequence at some stage then that number is called a happy number. For example, start with the number 7. By applying the above formula we get the following sequence: 7, 49, 97, 130, 10, 1. So 7 is a happy number. Other such happy numbers are 1, 7, 10, 13, 19, 23, 28, 31, 32, 44, 49, 68, 70, 79, 82, 86, 91, 94, 97, 100, ...

Numbers that are not happy numbers are called unhappy numbers.

A composite number such that the sum of the number's digits equals the sum of the digits of its distinct prime factors (excluding 1) is called a hoax number. The first few hoax numbers are 22, 58, 84, 85, 94, 136, 160, 166, 202, 234, and the corresponding sums of the digits are 4, 13, 12, 13, 13, 10, 7, 13, 4, 9, 7.

The largest known prime numbers are:

$2^{6,972,593} - 1$

$2^{3,021,377} - 1$

$2^{2,976,221} - 1$

The largest is over 2 million digits long! These primes were all discovered in the last 3 years; the search for large primes has accelerated with the help of several hundred people across the internet in a project called GIMPS (the Great Internet Mersenne Prime Search).

The decimal expansion of all rational numbers either terminates or ends up in a repetitive sequence of numbers. But if the denominator of the fraction representing that rational number is not divisible by three then the repeating sequence is divisible by 9. E.g. 1/7 = 0.142857142857142857. The repeating number 142857 is divisible by 9. 41/55 = 0.7454545. The repeating number 45 is divisible by 9.

∞

An *n*-digit number, which is the sum of the *n*th powers of its digits is called an *n*-narcissistic number. The smallest known narcissistic number is 153 which can be written as $153 = 1^3 + 5^3 + 3^3$. Other narcissistic numbers are 370, 371, 407, 1634, 8202, 9474 and so on.

∞

A pan-digital number is a decimal integer, which contains each of the digits from 0 to

9 (and whose leading digit must be non-zero). The first few pan-digital numbers are 1023456789, 1023456798, 1023456879, 1023456897, 1023456978 ... A 10-digit pan-digital number is always divisible by 9 since the sum of its digits will always be 45 and 45 is divisible by 9.

∞

An *n*-persistent number is a positive integer *k* which contains the digits 0 to 9 (i.e., is a pan-digital number), and for which 2k, 3k ... nk also share this property. The first few n-persistent numbers are 1023456789, 1023456879, 1023457689, 1023457869.

∞

A sum-product number is a number *n* such that the sum of *n*'s digits times the product of *n*'s digits is *n* itself. E.g.

$$135 = (1 + 3 + 5) \times (1 \times 3 \times 5)$$

Obviously, such a number must be divisible by its digits as well as the sum of its digits. There are only three such sum-product numbers, 1, 135 and 144.

An undulant number is a number of the form aba, abab, etc. The first few non-trivial undulants (with the stipulation that a is not equal to b) are 101, 121, 131, 141, 151, 161, 171, 181, 191, 202, 212. The first few undulating squares are 121, 484, 676, 69696.

Look at the following few numbers:

$$1260 = 21 \times 60$$
$$1395 = 15 \times 93$$
$$1435 = 35 \times 41$$
$$1530 = 30 \times 51$$
$$1827 = 21 \times 87$$
$$6880 = 80 \times 86$$

Each of these numbers is the product of its digits taken two at a time. Such numbers are called vampire numbers and the combination of digits, which when multiplied together gives the original number, are called its fangs. Thus, 1260 is a vampire number and 21 and 60 are its fangs.

∞

A number *n* is called wasteful if the number of digits in the prime factorisation of *n* (including powers) uses more digits than the number of digits in *n*. The first few wasteful numbers are 4, 6, 8, 9, 12, 18, 20, 22, 24 ...

∞

2 is the only even prime number.

∞

$135 = 1^1 + 3^2 + 5^3$

∞

136 is a very peculiar number. The sum of the cubes of its digits is $1^3 + 3^3 + 6^3 = 1 + 27 + 216 = 244$. Now $2^3 + 4^3 + 4^3 = 136$. This is the only number to exhibit such a property.

∞

$175 = 1^1 + 7^2 + 5^3$.

∞

$198 = 11 + 99 + 88$.

∞

$315 = (4 + 3)(4 + 1)(4 + 5)$.

∞

$450 = (5 + 4)(5 + 5)(5 + 0)$.

$518 = 5^1 + 1^2 + 8^3$.

540 is divisible by its reverse.

$594 = 1^5 + 2^9 + 3^4$.

$732 = 1^7 + 2^6 + 3^5 + 4^4 + 5^3 + 6^2 + 7^1$.

$746 = 1^7 + 2^4 + 3^6$.

$780 = (5 + 7)(5 + 8)(5 + 0)$.

810 is divisible by its reverse.

$986 = 1^9 + 2^8 + 3^6$.

1098 = 11 + 0 + 999 + 88.

1099 = 1 + 0 + 999 + 99.

Trivia

The decade of 1990 contained three prime numbers, 1993, 1997 and 1999. Since most prime numbers except 2 and 5 end in 1,3,7 or 9 this particular decade having three prime numbers is considered a prime rich decade.

∞

If you multiply 111,111,111 by 111,111,111 you get 12,345,678,987, 654,321.

∞

Pick any number from 1 to 7. Multiply this number by 2. Add 5. Multiply it by 50. If you have already had your birthday this year, add 1754. If you haven't, add 1753. Now subtract the four digit year that you were born in, e.g., 1978 from this number. You should have a three digit number: the first digit of this was your original number, the next two digits give your age.

Every whole number can be expressed as the sum of four perfect squares. E.g. $7 = 2^2 + 1^2 + 1^2 + 1^2$ or $15 = 3^2 + 2^2 + 1^2 + 1^2$.

∞

In 1202, Fibonacci propounded a very interesting theorem. If integers N and M can be written as a sum of two squares then so can their product. E.g. $2 = 1^2 + 1^2$ and $34 = 3^2 + 5^2$ then their product 68 can also be written in the same way. In fact $68 = 2^2 + 8^2$.

∞

Multiply 37,037 by any single number from 1 to 9, then multiply that number by 3. Every digit in the answer will be the same as that first single number. E.g. 37,037 x 5 = 185,185.

185,185 × 3 = 555,555

∞

Pi has been calculated to 2,260,321,363 digits. The billionth digit in Pi is 9.

∞

The sum of the first 32423 (which is a palindromic number) consecutive prime numbers is 5897230146 which is a pandigital number.

∞

18 is the only number that is twice the sum of its digits.

∞

25 is the smallest square that can be written as a sum of 2 squares.

∞

26 is the only number directly between a square and a cube.

27 is the largest number that is the sum of the digits of its cube.

40 is the only number whose letters, when it is spelt out, are in alphabetical order.

50 is the smallest number that can be written as the sum of 2 squares in 2 ways.

54 is the smallest number that can be written as the sum of 3 squares in 3 ways.

60 is the smallest number divisible by 1 through 6. That is probably why it was chosen as a base for time-keeping rather than the number 10. Decimal time was not

found to be convenient.

∞

65 is the smallest number that becomes square if its reverse is either added to or subtracted from it.

∞

81 is the square of the sum of its digits.

∞

87 is the sum of the squares of the first 4 prime numbers.

∞

$89 = 8^1 + 9^2$.

∞

100 is the smallest square which is also the sum of 4 consecutive cubes. $100 = 1 + 8 + 27 + 64 = 1^3 + 2^3 + 3^3 + 4^3$.

121 is the only square known of the form $1 + p + p^2 + p^3 + p^4$, where p is a prime number. $121 = 1 + 3 + 3^2 + 3^3 + 3^4$.

∞

$a = b$

$a^2 = ab$

$a^2 - b^2 = ab - b^2$

$(a+b)(a - b) = b(a - b)$

$a+b = b$

$2b = b$

$2 = 1$. This series of equations is given to prove that 2 = 1. Although this may appear correct there is a fallacy in this. At step 5 both sides have been divided by a – b. But a = b. So a – b = 0. And, no number can be divided by 0.

Word Connections

Eban numbers are the sequence of numbers whose names in English do not contain the letter 'e' (i.e. 'e' is banned). The name was coined by N. J. A. Sloane around 1990.

∞

The first few eban numbers are 2, 4, 6, 30, 32, 34, 36, 40, 42, 44, 46, 50, 52, 54, 56, 60, 62, 64, 66, 2000, 2002, 2004. These exclude one, three, five, seven, eight, nine, ten, eleven, twelve, etc. which contain the letter 'e'.

∞

In English, every odd number contains an 'e', so all eban numbers are even. But all even numbers are not eban. For example, eight is an even number but it is not an eban number.

∞

By way of analogy with the eban numbers, aban numbers are defined as numbers whose English names do not contain the letter 'a'. Since the word 'thousand' contains the letter 'a' but no smaller numbers do, all the numbers 1 – 999 are aban numbers.

∞

Similarly, iban numbers are defined as numbers whose English names do not contain the letter 'i' . The first few are 1, 2, 3, 4, 7, 10, 11, 12, 14, 17, 20, 21, 22, 23, 24, 27, 40. Since all the numbers greater than 1 million contain the word fraction 'illion' in them there are a finite number of iban numbers. In fact, there are exactly 30275 of them. The largest one is 777777.

∞

Oban numbers are defined as numbers whose English names do not contain the letter 'o'. The first few are 3, 5, 6, 7, 8, 9, 10, 11, 12, 13, 15, 16, 17, 18, 19, 20, 23, 25, 26.

∞

Uban numbers are defined as numbers whose English names do not contain the letter 'u'. The first few uban numbers are 1, 2, 3, 5, 6, 7, 8, 9, 10, 11, 12, 13, 15, 16, 17, 18, 19, 20, 21, 22, 23, 25, 26. Since the number 'four' contains the letter 'u' it is not an uban number. Therefore all the numbers that have 4 in them are excluded from the sequence of uban numbers. The only exception to this rule is the number 40. It has '4' in it but it is an uban number.

∞

The number 666 is notorious since it has been called 'the number of the beast' in the bible. It is also said there that it is the number of a man. However, the identity of that man is not revealed. So it is called the number of the Antichrist. Since various letters of the alphabet have been used to represent certain numbers many mathematicians have tried to find out if the letters representing the number 666 carry any specific meaning.

The ancient Greek word for 'the Latin speaking man' is *Lateinos*. If the letters of this word are converted to numbers according to the Greek system then the sum of those numbers is 666 (30 + 1 + 300 + 5 + 10 + 50 + 70 + 200 = 666).

∞

The ancient Greek word for 'The Latin Kingdom' is *'He Latine Basileia'*. The numbers represented by these letters also add up to 666. So do the Greek words for 'The Italian Church'. The number 666 is also called the Apocalypse number.

∞

A short mnemonic for remembering the first eight decimal digits of pi is: 'May I have a large container of coffee?' giving 3.1415926. 'But I must a while endeavour to reckon right' gives nine correct digits, 3.14159265. A more substantial mnemonic giving 15 digits, 3.14159265358979 is: 'How I want a drink, alcoholic of course, after the heavy lectures involving quantum mechanics,' originally coined by Sir James Jeans. A slight extension of this adds the phrase, 'All of thy geometry, Herr Planck, is fairly hard,' giving 24 digits in all 3.14159265358979323846264.

∞

In *Moralia,* the Greek biographer and philosopher Plutarch states, 'Chrysippus says that the number of compound propositions that can be made from only ten simple propositions exceeds a million. Hipparchus, to be sure, refuted this by showing that on the affirmative side there are 103049 compound statements, and on the negative side 310952.' The numbers in this quote are known as Plutarch numbers.

∞

The integer sequence beginning with a single digit in which the next term is obtained by describing the previous term is called a look-and-say sequence. Starting with 1, the sequence would be defined by '1, one 1, two 1s, one 2 one 1,' etc., and the result is 1, 11, 21, 1211, 111221, 312211, 13112221, 1113213211.

